FRANCIS FRITH'S
CAMBRIDGESHIRE
LIVING MEMORIES

LIZ CARTER is a local and family historian, dividing her time between professional research and lecturing on family, local and social history for the University of Cambridge, Institute of Continuing Education and the WEA. She has lived in Cambridgeshire for over 30 years during which time she has taken a deep interest in the local history and social development of the area. She is an active member of the local history and family history societies and is currently involved in a transcription project of her local church records and a book on World War One soldiers from the local area.

FRANCIS FRITH'S
PHOTOGRAPHIC MEMORIES

CAMBRIDGESHIRE
LIVING MEMORIES

LIZ CARTER

First published in the United Kingdom in 2004 by
Frith Book Company Ltd

Hardback Edition 2004
ISBN 1-85937-501-4

British Library Cataloguing in Publication Data

Francis Frith's Cambridgeshire - Living Memories
Liz Carter

Frith Book Company Ltd
Frith's Barn, Teffont,
Salisbury, Wiltshire SP3 5QP
Tel: +44 (0) 1722 716 376
Email: info@francisfrith.co.uk
www.francisfrith.co.uk

Printed and bound in Great Britain

Front Cover: HUNTINGDON, *High Street c1955* H136002
Frontispiece: WICKEN, *The Pond c1955* W493007

*The colour-tinting is for illustrative purposes only, and is not intended to be
historically accurate*

AS WITH ANY HISTORICAL DATABASE THE FRITH ARCHIVE IS CONSTANTLY
BEING CORRECTED AND IMPROVED, AND THE PUBLISHERS WOULD
WELCOME INFORMATION ON OMISSIONS OR INACCURACIES

CONTENTS

FRANCIS FRITH
VICTORIAN PIONEER

FRANCIS FRITH, founder of the world-famous photographic archive, was a complex and multi-talented man. A devout Quaker and a highly successful Victorian businessman, he was philosophical by nature and pioneering in outlook.

By 1855 he had already established a wholesale grocery business in Liverpool, and sold it for the astonishing sum of £200,000, which is the equivalent today of over £15,000,000. Now a very rich man, he was able to indulge his passion for travel. As a child he had pored over travel books written by early explorers, and his fancy and imagination had been stirred by family holidays to the sublime mountain regions of Wales and Scotland. 'What lands of spirit-stirring and enriching scenes and places!' he had written. He was to return to these scenes of grandeur in later years to 'recapture the thousands of vivid and tender memories', but with a different purpose. Now in his thirties, and captivated by the new science of photography, Frith set out on a series of pioneering journeys up the Nile and to the Near East that occupied him from 1856 unti 1860.

INTRIGUE AND EXPLORATION

These far-flung journeys were packed with intrigue and adventure. In his life story, written when he was sixty-three, Frith tells of being held captive by bandits, and of fighting 'an awful midnight battle to the very point of surrender with a deadly pack of hungry, wild dogs'. Wearing flowing Arab costume, Frith arrived at Akaba by camel sixty years before Lawrence of Arabia, where he encountered 'desert princes and rival sheikhs, blazing with jewel-hilted swords'.

He was the first photographer to venture beyond the sixth cataract of the Nile. Africa was still the mysterious 'Dark Continent', and Stanley and Livingstone's historic meeting was a decade into the future. The conditions for picture taking confound belief. He laboured for hours in his wicker dark-room in the sweltering heat of the desert, while the volatile chemicals fizzed dangerously in their trays. Back in London he exhibited his photographs and was 'rapturously cheered' by members of the Royal Society. His reputation as a photographer was made overnight.

VENTURE OF A LIFE-TIME

Characteristically, Frith quickly spotted the opportunity to create a new business as a specialist publisher of photographs. He lived in an era of immense and sometimes violent change. For the poor in the early part of Victoria's reign work was exhausting and the hours long, and people had precious little free time to enjoy themselves. Most people had no transport other than a cart or gig at their disposal, and rarely

business one only has to look at the catalogue issued by Frith & Co in 1886: it runs to some 670 pages, listing not only many thousands of views of the British Isles but also many photographs of most European countries, and China, Japan, the USA and Canada - note the sample page shown on page 9 from the hand-written Frith & Co ledgers recording the pictures. By 1890 Frith had created the greatest specialist photographic publishing company in the world, with over 2,000 sales outlets - more than the combined number that Boots and WH Smith have today! The picture on the next page shows the Frith & Co display board at Ingleton in the Yorkshire Dales (left of window). Beautifully constructed with a mahogany frame and gilt inserts, it could display up to a dozen local scenes.

POSTCARD BONANZA

The ever-popular holiday postcard we know today took many years to develop. In 1870 the Post Office issued the first plain cards, with a pre-printed stamp on one face. In 1894 they allowed other publishers' cards to be sent through the mail with an attached adhesive halfpenny stamp. Demand grew rapidly, and in 1895 a new size of postcard was permitted called the court card, but there was little room for illustration. In 1899, a year after Frith's death, a new card measuring 5.5 x 3.5 inches became the standard format, but it was not until 1902 that the divided back came into being, so that the address and message could be on one face and a full-size illustration on the other. Frith & Co were in the vanguard of postcard development: Frith's sons Eustace and Cyril continued their father's monumental task, expanding the number of views offered to the public and recording more and more places in Britain, as the coasts and countryside were opened up to mass travel.

Francis Frith had died in 1898 at his villa in Cannes, his great project still growing. The archive he created continued in business for another seventy years. By 1970 it contained over a third of a million pictures showing 7,000 British towns and villages.

travelled far beyond the boundaries of their own town or village. However, by the 1870s the railways had threaded their way across the country, and Bank Holidays and half-day Saturdays had been made obligatory by Act of Parliament. All of a sudden the working man and his family were able to enjoy days out and see a little more of the world.

With typical business acumen, Francis Frith foresaw that these new tourists would enjoy having souvenirs to commemorate their days out. In 1860 he married Mary Ann Rosling and set out on a new career: his aim was to photograph every city, town and village in Britain. For the next thirty years he travelled the country by train and by pony and trap, producing fine photographs of seaside resorts and beauty spots that were keenly bought by millions of Victorians. These prints were painstakingly pasted into family albums and pored over during the dark nights of winter, rekindling precious memories of summer excursions.

THE RISE OF FRITH & CO

Frith's studio was soon supplying retail shops all over the country. To meet the demand he gathered about him a small team of photographers, and published the work of independent artist-photographers of the calibre of Roger Fenton and Francis Bedford. In order to gain some understanding of the scale of Frith's

FRANCIS FRITH'S LEGACY

Frith's legacy to us today is of immense significance and value, for the magnificent archive of evocative photographs he created provides a unique record of change in the cities, towns and villages throughout Britain over a century and more. Frith and his fellow studio photographers revisited locations many times down the years to update their views, compiling for us an enthralling and colourful pageant of British life and character.

We are fortunate that Frith was dedicated to recording the minutiae of everyday life. For it is this sheer wealth of visual data, the painstaking chronicle of changes in dress, transport, street layouts, buildings, housing, engineering and landscape that captivates us so much today. His remarkable images offer us a powerful link with the past and with the lives of our ancestors.

THE VALUE OF THE ARCHIVE TODAY

Computers have now made it possible for Frith's many thousands of images to be accessed almost instantly. Frith's images are increasingly used as visual resources, by social historians, by researchers into genealogy and ancestry, by architects and town planners, and by teachers involved in local history projects.

In addition, the archive offers every one of us an opportunity to examine the places where we and our families have lived and worked down the years. Highly successful in Frith's own era, the archive is now, a century and more on, entering a new phase of popularity. Historians consider the Francis Frith Collection to be of prime national importance. It is the only archive of its kind remaining in private ownership. Francis Frith's archive is now housed in an historic timber barn in the beautiful village of Teffont in Wiltshire. Its founder would not recognize the archive office as it is today. In place of the many thousands of dusty boxes containing glass plate negatives and an all-pervading odour of photographic chemicals, there are now ranks of computer screens. He would be amazed to watch his images travelling round the world at unimaginable speeds through internet lines.

The archive's future is both bright and exciting. Francis Frith, with his unshakeable belief in making photographs available to the greatest number of people, would undoubtedly approve of what is being done today with his lifetime's work. His photographs depicting our shared past are now bringing pleasure and enlightenment to millions around the world a century and more after his death.

CAMBRIDGESHIRE LIVING MEMORIES

AN INTRODUCTION

IN THE 1950s the area now known as CAMBRIDGESHIRE comprised four distinct areas: two ancient counties, Huntingdonshire and Cambridgeshire, the Soke of Peterborough, and the Isle of Ely. In 1965 the Soke of Peterborough, an independent authority since 1888, was combined with Huntingdonshire. On 1 April 1974 Huntingdonshire was merged with Cambridgeshire and the Isle of Ely, the new county being known as Cambridgeshire. In the 1990s there was a move to separate Huntingdonshire again, following the success of

GRANTCHESTER, *Byron's Pool c1955* G44009

10

Rutland, but the best that could be achieved were Huntingdonshire District Council signs strategically placed on the old county boundaries.

The Town Development Act of 1952, aimed at reducing overcrowding in London, led to the rapid growth of many towns in the area. The post-war building boom revived the local brick-making businesses: over 600 million bricks per year were being produced at the Fletton works in the 1960s, whilst the belching chimneys of the Whittlesey brickworks, now part of the Hanson Group, are a landmark for miles around. The worked-out brickpits at Fletton have been used as landfill, and now form the new suburb of Hampton. Peterborough's population has increased dramatically in the last 25 years owing to overspill from London, and it now has a large multi-ethnic community.

The local railways suffered with the Beeching cuts; the link between St Ives and Cambridge disappeared, along with all the local branch lines linking small rural communities. It is only in the last 20 years that the improved train timetables have enabled commuters to settle in the remoter rural areas, turning many of the small villages into dormitories for London and Cambridge. There is even talk now of bringing back the St Ives/Cambridge train using a coach system on the old rail track to ease the congestion on the local roads.

The two counties have always had a good road system dating from the Roman period. With the

HUNTINGDON, *High Street c1955* H136002

11

increase in road use over the last 50 years, major changes have taken place. The original route of the A1 dates back to pre-Roman times, but it was not until 1936 that it was recognised as a single road of over 400 miles linking London with Edinburgh. It quickly acquired the name of the Great North Road, and it remained the principal route north until the opening of the M1 in 1958. The road was upgraded in the 1980s, and the modern dual carriageway A1 and A1M now bypasses all the major communities such as St Neots, Buckden, Huntingdon and Peterborough.

The other major cross-county route, the old A604, has also been upgraded to dual carriageway. Work at the Cambridge end took place in the 1970s (I have fond memories of the road-works whilst trying to get to the maternity unit in Cambridge!) and the road number was changed to A14. This road now links the M1 to the M11. The last major road development is the M11, which links London and Stansted Airport with Cambridge.

Up to the 1940s the main local industries were brick and tile making, brewing, farming, iron founding and printing. By 1963 new industries had appeared, including light engineering, electronics, plastics and specialist paper products. Sugar processing at Woodston near Peterborough and a chicory factory at St Ives showed the change in agriculture. Science Parks have sprung up around Cambridge town, now recognised as one of the leading areas for computer technology.

LINTON, *The Church c1955* L459022

Farming is still a major industry in the area, but following the foot and mouth epidemic, there is more evidence of diversification.

Echoes of the Second World War remain in the large number of disused airfields still to be found around the county. Some, such as Brampton, have been retained by the Royal Air Force, although they are no longer operational bases. Others, such as Warboys, have reverted to agricultural use, whilst others have been leased to the USAF. Molesworth was the site of major protests against Cruise missiles in the 1980s. Conington, once home to the mighty B52 bombers, is now a private airfield, whilst the future of Alconbury airfield is the subject of much local and national debate.

The Fenland drainage system attempts to keep the land dry, but climate change and unconsidered building development have brought disaster to many new communities, with major flooding in St Ives, Cambridge and St Neots occurring twice within recent years. The Washes, designed to accommodate surplus water, are submerged more and more often. Ice-skating on the frozen flooded wastes at Whittlesey and Bluntisham still take place after hard frosts.

There is a gradual change in the landscape as we move away from Huntingdon alongside the lazy River Ouse, down the permanently congested A14 towards the bustling conurbation of Cambridge. Looking north-east towards Wisbech, we find the wide open skies and water-lined fields of Fenland, whilst to the south are the gentle rolling slopes and winding hedges of the clay upland leading down to Essex and over to Suffolk. Wherever we look, the landscape is steeped in legend - the last sixty years is but a paragraph in the continuing history of the area.

FROM SOUTH TO NORTH -
UP THE GREAT NORTH ROAD

The town of St Neots was first recorded in 1156, and its lasting success is due to the market granted in the 12th century to be held between the bridge and the priory gates. We follow the old route north, with a detour to look at the famous village of Kimbolton with its castle; then we visit the Bishop of Lincoln's palace at Buckden. Throughout our journey, the echoes of an earlier coaching age remind us that this was once the major north/south route between London and Edinburgh. We reach the end our journey north at Castor, a small village built near the Roman pottery centre of Durobrivae.

ST NEOTS, *High Street c1955* S37001

We enter St Neots over the bridge straight into the market place. The Cross Keys Hotel (left) overlooked the market up to the 1980s, when major development was undertaken; whilst the facade has been retained, the hotel is now a shopping mall.

15

ST NEOTS
Market Square 1965
S37043

Here we see a traditional busy Thursday market scene; a farmer's market has also recently started on a Saturday. The Bridge Hotel, the white-painted building to the left, is now a Beefeater pub, and Boots (centre right) has become Lloyds, reflecting a prosperous retail shopping centre.

ST NEOTS, *High Street 1960* s37029

Looking back down towards the market square in the distance, this view shows the old High Street prior to the 1980s modernisation. The sign on the left refers to the ancient bridge over the River Ouse; after much debate, the old bridge was replaced by a modern concrete structure.

▲ **ST NEOTS**
Roper's Shop c1965 S37060

A child's paradise in the 1960s, this shop still stands just over the crossroads on the Huntingdon Road out of St Neots. It has since been a newsagents and video rental shop, and is now a fast food outlet for USA Chicken.

▼ **GREAT STAUGHTON,** *The Highway looking East c1955* G279012

The White Hart on the left is the only pub left in the village. When the bicycle shop, just past the memorial (left), closed in the 1960s Frank Croach, the butcher, moved in. Although he died in 1990, there is still a butcher's shop here.

► **GREAT STAUGHTON**
The Highway c1955
G279004

Looking towards Kimbolton, this view shows the old chapel, which was converted to a private dwelling in 2000. The Red Lion Hotel beyond it has gone, now replaced by Red Lion Court, and Mrs Odell now runs the new post office (to the left of the chapel) - the old one closed in 2000.

KIMBOLTON
The Village c1955
K157003

This is the High Street, the main street in Kimbolton. The George Hotel is now a private house. The garage beyond it, with a fake timber-framed frontage, has long gone. Local sources state that the timber frame was indeed a fake - the battens were held in place by old football boot studs!

▶ **KIMBOLTON**
High Street c1955
K157012

We are looking back towards the castle, now Kimbolton School. The Reverend Lancaster, famous for his firework displays, now occupies the end cottage, and Kimbolton House on the right, the site of the school before it moved to the castle, now houses a playgroup. Kimbolton was voted Best Kept Village in 1989.

▶ **KIMBOLTON**
East Street c1965
K157058

This narrow back street, running parallel to the High Street, has changed a little. The Half Moon pub (right) has gone, and there are traffic-calming bumps here now. Harold White, a builder, used to live here - he built the yellow brick houses near the station, known as 'White City'.

◀ **KIMBOLTON**
Church Corner c1955
K157010

Flanders and Sons, builders and coffin makers, occupied the large house on the left until recently. There was talk of redeveloping the site, but fortunately it has not changed apart from the volume of traffic, which would make it dangerous to stand in the street to reproduce this photograph!

▲ **BUCKDEN,** *Grafham Water c1965* B237036

Grafham Water is a reservoir for Anglia Water, constructed between 1962 and 1965, covering 2½ square miles - one of the largest lakes in England. To the west of Buckden, it is home to a sailing club and watersports centre.

◄**BUCKDEN**
The Village c1950 B237012

Returning to the Great North Road, we come to Buckden. The new A1 by-pass means that this village has become a quiet backwater, but signs of modern development can nowadays be seen - a housing estate has replaced the brick wall on the left.

▶ **BUCKDEN**
High Street c1955
B237017

This is the heart of the village, with the George Inn (left) and the Lion Hotel, both former coaching inns, standing opposite each other. The shops have definitely changed in recent years; you can now kit yourself from the skin out with lingerie, shoes and high class couture, whilst a One Stop Store provides for more basic needs.

◀ **BUCKDEN**
The Lion Hotel c1955
B237015

The Lion Hotel was famous as a coaching inn in the 18th and 19th centuries. There have been changes to the facade - there are now flower beds and car parking at the front. The Trust House sign disappeared when the hotel left the group in the 1980s.

◄ **BUCKDEN**
The Great Tower c1950
B237009

The Great Tower, dating from the 15th century, has seen many different tenants, including, briefly, a post office! In 1957 it was taken over by the Claretian Missionaries, and under their care the Catholic church of St Hugh of Lincoln was built in 1959. Nowadays it is a Roman Catholic retreat, and it is also used by many different local groups as a meeting place.

◄ **BUCKDEN**
The River Ouse c1960
B237029

We are taking a detour out of Buckden to the Offords; the Offord & Buckden Anglers Club now have a car park and hut here. The water authorities carried out work on the two weirs in the 1990s to prevent undermining of the river bank, and new metal bridges have appeared.

◀ BRAMPTON
Church Hill c1965
B182010

Continuing through the village, we come to The Black Bull public house (centre); the parish church stands in the background. The large double doors on the right-hand side of the pub have been blocked off and a window installed to provide more bar space.

◄ BRAMPTON
*The Camp
Entrance c1965*
B182022

The thatched
cottage was the
original gatehouse
for Brampton Park,
which became RAF
Brampton in the
Second World War.
The water towers
were demolished
in the early 1990s
when a new gate
with a mini-
roundabout was
built.

▲ BRAMPTON, *The Church c1955* B182018

The original Norman church was rebuilt in the 14th century and dedicated to St Mary
Magdalene. The tower was rebuilt in 1635 and a modern Lady Chapel was added in 1920; its
roof is lined with heraldic shields.

◄ BRAMPTON
The Green c1960
B182005

The green, on the far side
of the village from the
church and overlooked by
the village school, is now
enclosed with a low
wooden fence. Beyond the
thatched cottages the
Methodist chapel still
attracts a large
congregation, whilst the
roadway becomes
jammed with cars at
school times.

▼ **STILTON,** *The Bell Hotel c1955* S673021

This famous coaching inn was one of 14 inns or ale-houses in the village in the 19th century. When the A1 by-pass was opened in 1959 the village declined; the Bell closed in 1963, almost becoming derelict. New owners in the 1980s brought a fresh lease of life, and it is now a popular hotel and conference centre.

▶ **STILTON**

High Street c1955 S673019

The Stilton Cheese public house takes it name from the famous blue cheese. It is actually made in nearby counties, and was originally brought to Stilton for shipment south by coach. When the old telephone box (centre) was moved and placed next to the village pump, it had to be listed to prevent its being replaced with a modern 'shower cubicle' version!

◄ **STILTON**
High Street c1955
S673009

Looking north, this view shows the old Great North Road before the new A1 bypass. Note the bollards in the centre of the road - an early form of traffic calming - which were subsequently removed. Local inhabitants have requested their return for safety reasons.

▶ **STILTON**
High Street c1955
S673010

It is hard to believe that there is an annual cheese-rolling charity race with local teams, many in fancy dress, bowling a 'cheese' (usually a log cut and painted to represent a Stilton cheese) along this part of the High Street. The winning team receives a crate of beer and a real cheese.

▲ **CASTOR,** *The Church c1955* C584017

Our journey up the Great North Road ends here. The church, dedicated in 1124 to St Kyneburga, the third of four daughters of Peada, King of Mercia and founder of the abbey at Peterborough, stands on a slight rise overlooking the village of Castor and the River Nene.

▶ **CASTOR**
Peterborough Road c1955 C584012

This scene has changed little in the past 50 years, apart from the Royal Oak (left) losing its hanging sign and side entrance in the 1980s after a couple of lorries demolished the porch! The pub garden has extended out to the side road, and a petanque pitch has appeared where the tree stood behind the railings, on the left.

FROM WEST TO EAST -
PETERBOROUGH TO WISBECH

Heading east at Castor we come to the city of Peterborough, which has expanded dramatically in recent years. Taking the A47 east, we reach Thorney, built around the medieval abbey, before heading off into the Fens, with their characteristic flat landscape and open skies. Our first stop is Whittlesey, a thriving market town, well known for the Straw Bear parade in early January. Heading east again along the A605 we arrive at March. March, like Whittlesey, is a bustling market town built in medieval times and situated on the old river Nene, which gave it early prosperity. From March we head north to cross over the new River Nene and follow the side road through Wisbech St Mary into Wisbech - 'Queen of the Fens'. Wisbech, well known in earlier times as a trading port and used more recently as a backdrop for the film *Revolution*, was home to the Peckover family and Octavia Hill, the social reformer. Just a short step away from Wisbech is Leverington, where we end our journey eastwards.

PETERBOROUGH, *Church Street c1955* P47048

Between the parish church of St John and the Guildhall was the old police station (right), demolished in 1963 when the old Market Place was revamped. This busy street scene is nowadays replaced by occasional delivery vans and taxis, because the lower half of Church Street has been closed to through traffic.

31

PETERBOROUGH
Market Square c1955
P47012

The weekly market held in the old Market Square was moved in October 1963 to the site of the old cattle market behind Broadway. Now, instead of market stalls, brass bands and musical roundabouts appear at weekends.

PETERBOROUGH, *Cathedral Square and the Guildhall c1965* P47071

Here we have the old Market Square, renamed Cathedral Square in 1963. It has been pedestrianised with trees, imitation gas globe lights and CCTV, with Starbucks occupying the old Lloyds Bank building (extreme right) and an opticians shop in lieu of E J Gibbs on the corner ahead.

PETERBOROUGH, *The Town Hall c1955* P47017

The only real change to this scene is that now there are no cars - the whole of Bridge Street up to Cathedral Square has been closed to traffic and paved over. Occasional collectors' fairs or exhibitions are held in the Town Hall which, despite its classical lines, was only built in 1930.

▼ **PETERBOROUGH,** *The River Nene 1952* P47041

Over the Town Bridge, which forms the old county boundary, the power station has been replaced with a shopping centre. In the foreground, a paved riverside walkway lined with willow trees nowadays leads up to the Grain Barge Chinese restaurant.

▶ **THORNEY**
The River c1955 T33012

This stream is crossed by the major A47 in the distance, now controlled by traffic lights owing to the large volume of traffic. Until 1910 the village was part of the estate of the Duke of Bedford, who was responsible for many of the buildings on the High Street.

WHITTLESEY
Market Street c1965
W90003

This view down Market Street shows how Whittlesey has prospered in the past fifty years. The right-hand side of Market Street has been redeveloped, with the Queens Head replaced by the Market Street Cafe and a hairdresser's shop. Further along, shops have taken over the garage, but the cycle shop remains.

WHITTLESEY
Market Place c1965
W90005

Dating from 1680, the Butter Cross, now a listed building, provides the focal point for the busy Friday market, now with new metal railings and seating. Most of the shops around the square have changed in the past ten years, including the thatched greengrocer's shop to the left of the Butter Cross, now a cab company and insurance office.

▼ **WHITTLESEY,** *The Memorial c1965* W90016

The war memorial to the men of two world wars also includes W G Greenwood, who died in 1951 in Korea. The NatWest Bank now occupies the left-hand corner building, whilst on the right the street was completely redeveloped in the 1980s with estate agents' offices and Lloyds Bank.

▶ **MARCH**

The Fountain c1955

M28048

This ornate fountain was erected in 1912 and cost £180; it was the subject of much public debate. It remains today, painted an eye-catching green and yellow, at the busy junction at the top of Broad Street, whilst the Wheel public house (left) was demolished in 1980 to make way for flats.

◄ MARCH
The High Street
c1955 M28013

Ye Olde Griffin is the oldest hotel in March, dating from 1793 and originally a coaching inn with its own brewery on site! In the background the Corn Exchange tower presides over the market place, where a market is still held on Wednesdays.

MARCH
The High Street c1955
M28014

This view looks up towards the market place and the bridge. The photographer was probably standing outside the old school, now the home of the March & District Museum.

▲ WISBECH ST MARY
High Street c1960 W492012

Heading north-east we come to Wisbech St Mary, which is built alongside the New River, which takes the water of the Nene to the huge pumping station at Denver Sluice. The banks of this river tower over most of the buildings in the village, such is the shrinkage of the local peat landscape.

▶ WISBECH ST MARY
The Bridge Inn c1960 W492014

The Bridge Inn still stands on the corner, and although now rendered and painted white with new windows, it is easily identified with the building we see in the photograph.

WISBECH, *The Clarkson Memorial c1955* W115023

This famous local monument, designed by Sir Gilbert Scott, was erected in 1881 to commemorate Thomas Clarkson, an active anti-slavery campaigner. In 1996 his efforts were given national recognition when a memorial plaque was placed in Westminster Abbey. The background buildings have hardly changed, except that the Belfast Shop now replaces Fell's wireless shop overlooking the monument (extreme left).

▶ WISBECH
Market Place c1955 W115045

These two photographs show the
market place over a span of ten years.
The Fifty Shilling Tailor, facing us, has
reverted to John Collier, J E Hall next
door have removed the large sign
from their building, and some of the
street furniture has changed, but
overall the scene has not changed
dramatically. In 1988 the whole area
was redeveloped and pedestrianised,
and some shops vanished, including
J E Hall and the Ship Hotel (right,
W115091 on page 41). A market is
still held on Thursday and Saturday -
during the re-paving in 1996, the
market was held in a local car park.
The Rose & Crown Hotel (left of John
Collier), which was featured in the
BBC's recent adaptation of *Martin
Chuzzlewit*, is still popular, and when
the Talbot Hotel was renovated
recently, a skeleton was found
bricked up in a wall!

◄ **WISBECH**
Market Place c1965
W115091

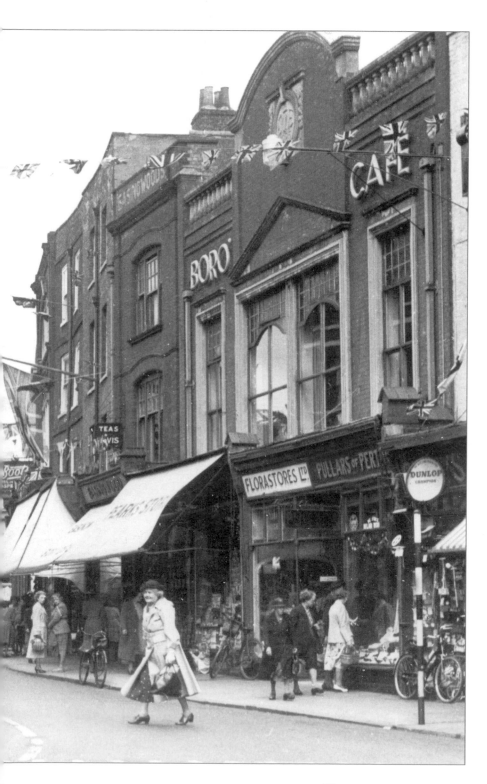

WISBECH
High Street c1955
W115046

The most striking change comes with the pedestrianisation of this area and the erection of a wrought iron archway, proclaiming the High Street. Most of the shops have been rebuilt, and well-known names, such as Boots the chemist (right), have moved to the new Horsefair Centre.

▲ **WISBECH**
The Canal c1955 W115020

▶ **WISBECH**
The Hope Inn c1955 W115019

These two pictures are an echo of the commercial waterways of the past. The whole area shown in these two photographs vanished when the new bridge over the river and the new Churchill Road were built to ease congestion in the town centre in 1971. The new Somerfield supermarket now stands on the site of the old Hope Inn.

44

WISBECH
Leach's Mill c1955 W115024

The top half of this mill tower was demolished, along with the other factory buildings, leaving a stumpy tower, which has been modernised. The whole area around the mill has been developed, and the road in the foreground is now a dual carriageway with pedestrian-controlled traffic lights.

LEVERINGTON
The Six Ringers c1965
L451010

The Six Ringers was built in 1913; over the past 35 years it has hardly changed except for new windows and a new front door. Leylandii trees line the nearside of the plot, but the view down the road remains very pastoral.

LEVERINGTON, *Gorefield Road c1960* L451017

Essentially little has changed in this picture. The tree-lined road still runs straight past the refurbished village hall in the distance, whilst the building hidden behind the trees on the left was demolished and the site redeveloped as a small housing estate.

FROM ABBEY TO ABBEY -
THE FENLAND EDGES

Starting off from Littleport, famous as the birthplace of Harley Davison of motorbike fame, we arrive in Ely, with its abbey and cathedral overlooking the fens. From Ely we keep to the high ground, coming to Sutton with its pepperpot church, said to be modeled on Ely, and then to Haddenham. Dropping down into the fens, we take the route of the old causeway to arrive at Earith - situated on the River Ouse, this village has a long and chequered history. The neighbouring village of Bluntisham is well known as the home of Dorothy L Sayers, the author. Somersham, our next stop, was the site of the Bishop of Ely's palace in early times, and has the distinction of having the Greenwich Meridian running right through the middle of the town. From Somersham it is a short step to Warboys, probably best remembered for the Pathfinder Squadrons of World War II. We end our journey at Ramsey, known in earlier times as Ramsey the Golden because of its prosperous abbey, now part of the local senior school. Unlike March and Whittlesey, this ancient market town has not thrived in recent years - many of its shops now stand empty.

LITTLEPORT, *The Bridge c1960* L366016

This concrete bridge replaced the earlier iron bridge in 1959 as part of the flood prevention scheme that started in the late 1950s. Whilst the bridge was being constructed, the Great River Ouse Board provided a chain punt as a pedestrian ferry.

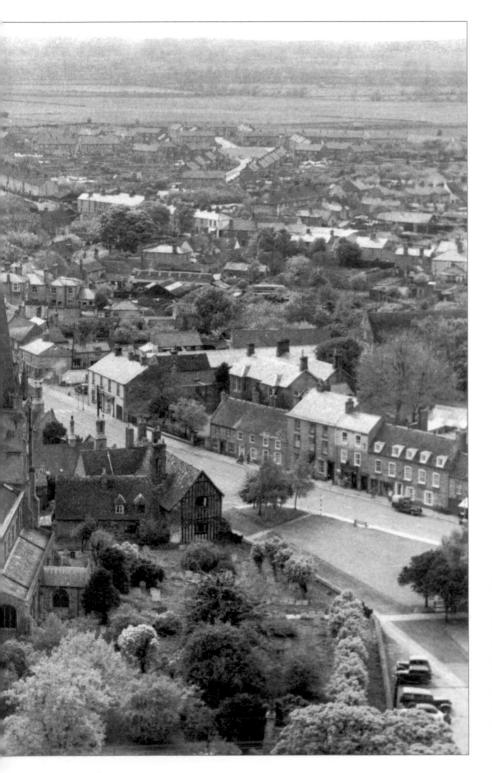

ELY
The View from the West Tower c1955 E34068

We are looking down on St Mary's Church. The distant green fields and trees are now replaced by in-fill housing. A survey of the cathedral's west tower in 1971 found serious structural problems, and repairs costing over £500,000 were undertaken in 1974.

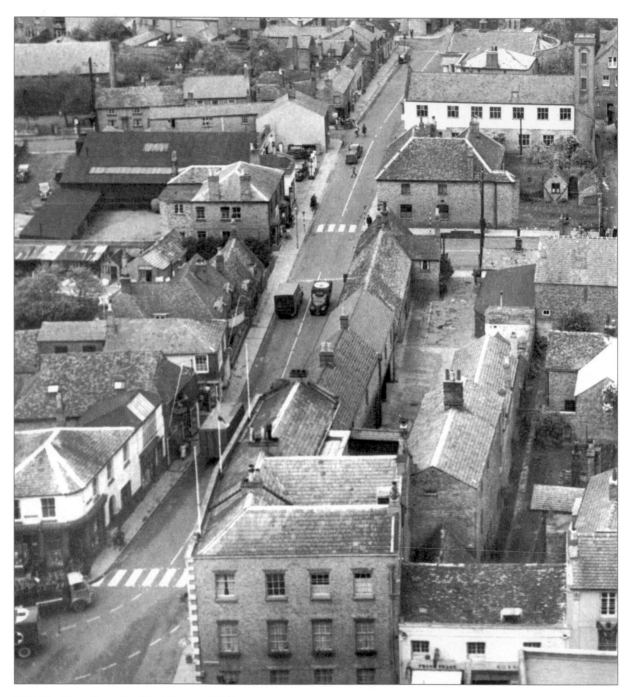

ELY, *The View from the West Tower c1955* E34074

The two ambulances (centre), identified by the crosses on their roofs, are probably en route from the Royal Air Force Hospital in Lynn Road. It was closed after the Gulf War and reopened as the Princess of Wales Memorial Hospital in the late 1980s.

ELY
Cromwell House and St Mary's Church c1955 E34010

The house occupied by Oliver Cromwell whilst he was governor of the Isle of Ely between 1636 and 1647 was at one time the vicarage for St Mary's Church, and is now the Ely Tourist Information Centre. As well as the usual tourist information, the centre runs an Ely ghost tour, and has a wealth of information about the Lord Protector.

ELY, *The Cathedral, the West Front c1955* E34011

The magnificent west front of the cathedral overlooks the Cannon Green; since this picture was taken the fence has been replaced by a new wall. In 1986 massive restoration work was required. An appeal raised £4 million in just one year, and the work was completed by 1990.

▶ **SUTTON**
High Street c1955
S674003

Oats Lane on the left, named after the Oats family who for many generations were the local millers, is still a narrow by-road, but the Green in the distance has been developed with a One Stop shop, a bus stop and a telephone box.

◀ **SUTTON**
High Street c1955
S674028

Here on the left is the old post office before it moved to the Green. The library beside it has now expanded to fill the whole building. In the distance, Nunns the outfitter has been replaced by an Indian takeaway restaurant. Both the Crown and the George & Dragon public houses (on the right-hand side of the street) have ceased trading, and are now private dwellings.

▲ **HADDENHAM,** *The Green c1950* H249006

The green now boasts a locally crafted village sign, and no parking is allowed! On one side of the green the Baptist chapel is still active, but the Chequers pub and Lloyds Bank (right) have gone, and the old Baptist Hall is now the new health centre.

◄ **HADDENHAM**
West End c1950 H249005

Driving through West End, the visitor is reminded of the Dutch engineers who were brought over to work on the fenland drainage and for whom some of the terraced cottages were built. I wonder how many villagers had televisions in 1950 - note the number of aerials in this picture.

▲ EARITH

The River Ouse c1955 E201021

These boats moored in the Cut show how the commercial river trade of earlier times has now given way to pleasure boating. Messing about on the water has always been popular at Earith, with the Riverside Hotel, the Crown Hotel and the new marina all offering facilities for boating and fishing enthusiasts.

► EARITH

High Street c1955 E201024

The George & Dragon public house in the foreground (left) was demolished in 1964 to allow very long concrete pillars to be transported around the corner. These were for the track constructed between Earith and Sutton Gault for the hovercraft test bed. The site, now occupied by the decorative village sign, is still referred to as George Corner.

▲ **EARITH,** *West End c1955* E201023

Jewson & Son the timber merchants - nowadays better known as 'The Jewson Lot' - started their business here in Earith in the 19th century, using the River Ouse to transport their timber. They moved to St Ives in 1988, and their site (the sheds and large building, left), which was derelict for many years, has now been redeveloped with Dutch-style houses in a courtyard setting.

◄ **BLUNTISHAM**
The Memorial and Main Road c1960
B726042

The war memorial at the junction of Hollidays Road and the main Earith to St Ives road was moved in early 1976 after a lorry hit it. It is now sited on the grass to the right of the picture, and has been replaced with a flowerbed.

▲ **BLUNTISHAM**
The Village Square c1965 B726035

This scene, with Lieutenant Colonel Tebbutt's 19th-century barograph under the shelter in front of the village shop has hardly changed. The shop, now run by Tony Rowell, is a veritable Aladdin's cave, and the two enamel advertisements still remain on the wall.

▲ **BLUNTISHAM,** *High Street c1955*
B726007

We are standing almost at the corner of the High Street, with the old rectory (home of the famous authoress Dorothy Sayers) hidden behind the wall on the right. Behind the trees on the right is the gardener's cottage, with the tradesmen's entrance to the rectory around the side.

◄ **BLUNTISHAM,** *The Chapel c1955*
B726008

The Baptists have been recorded in Bluntisham since the mid 17th century; a Meeting House was built on this site in 1787, and rebuilt in 1874. With bright blue woodwork set against locally made bricks, this is an eye-catching building. The railings in the foreground were recently replaced with a brick wall.

BLUNTISHAM
Colne Road c1955
B726010

We are looking towards Colne with the road up to the Heath on the left. The thatched cottage on the left was until recently home to the village carpenter and funeral director. Two new housing developments have appeared further down the road.

BLUNTISHAM, *Wood End c1955* B726014

Heading up to the old Heath, we leave the village through Wood End. This area has been recently developed with new housing on the right and Blacksmith's End, a modern development, on the left. The garage has also gone, to be replaced by a bungalow.

SOMERSHAM, *High Street c1965* S672026

The ancient Butter Cross became unsafe and was replaced in 2000 by a wrought iron replica with seating. Both the Rose and Crown (left) and the George (right) public houses thrive, but the corner shop (left, beyond the Rose and Crown), in this photograph Norman the grocer's, has led a chequered life, being at varying times a double-glazing shop, a DIY store with videos, and presently an estate agent's.

▶ **SOMERSHAM**
The Cross c1955 S672015

This view was taken standing against the old Butter Cross looking down the St Ives road. Bonnetts the bakers continue to trade from the same shop on the right-hand side of the road, down from the Rose and Crown - it is here that the local councillor, Miss Hettie Skeggs, used to send her dog with a basket to collect her bread; he would return with the bread and her change!

◄ **SOMERSHAM**
Church Street c1955
S672004

The Millennium Stone, a natural stone boulder underneath which lie two time capsules from the local school and the Baptist chapel, was placed on the left-hand side of the street to mark both the millennium and the Greenwich Meridian, which runs through Somersham.

SOMERSHAM
From the Church Tower c1960 S672003

Looking west towards Pidley cum Fenton, we see Somersham before the start of the building programme which has brought an industrial estate and several large housing developments. Fortunately the allotments in the foreground and the town football pitch have survived unscathed.

SOMERSHAM, *Bank Houses c1960* S672012

We are looking down the Chatteris road, where very little has changed in the past 40 years. The busy railway station situated just behind the photographer closed after the Beeching cuts of the 1960s, and this part of Somersham quietly faded into obscurity with no new development after the pre-war housing on the left.

SOMERSHAM, *Feoffees Road c1960* S672019

Named after the local charity, which has existed since medieval times, this council housing estate built in the late 1950s has remained unchanged. The long building at the end of the cul-de-sac, now Windsor Court, is a home for the elderly.

► **WARBOYS,** *The Church c1955*
W508014

Every year up to 2002 a special service has been held in the parish church for the Pathfinder Squadrons which flew from Warboys airfield in the Second World War. A beautiful stained glass window has been dedicated to them.

▼ **RAMSEY,** *Great Whyte c1955*
R359037

Ramsey in the 1950s was a thriving Fenland town, but it has now declined. Barclays Bank (right) still stands on the corner of Little Whyte, but the other traders have all gone. The last to go was Freeman & Sons, a tobacconist and newsagent's (left), which is now a card shop.

► **RAMSEY**
Great Whyte c1955
R359023

In the middle of Great Whyte stands the 'dummy clock'. Erected by public subscription in memory of Edward Fellowes, first Baron de Ramsey, it has recently been completely refurbished. Few people realise that the culverted Bury Brook runs under the Great Whyte, as the Gas Board recently discovered by accidentally drilling through the roof!

◄ **RAMSEY**
High Street c1955
R359016

The Horse and Gate pub (left) has been redeveloped into shops, the Lion Hotel (right) is now flats, and parking is only allowed on the left-hand side of the street. The one constant is the bank, now NatWest, at the junction of Great Whyte and the High Street, built over the Bury Brook.

COUNTY TOWN TO COUNTY TOWN - HUNTINGDON TO CAMBRIDGE AVOIDING THE A14

We start in Huntingdon, and crossing the old bridge, arrive in Godmanchester, site of an old Roman town. Hemingford Grey, Houghton and St Ives are all sited along the River Ouse, and along with Fenstanton and Hilton, provide ideal dormitories for commuters to London using the high-speed train connection from Huntingdon. The whole area has also been developed with tourism in mind, with waymarked walks, boating marinas and village trails. Moving away from the main road, we visit the villages of Swavesey, Willingham, and Over - but the name is a misnomer, since there is no way over the river at Over, the nearest crossing being at either St Ives or Earith. In earlier days there was a ferry to take passengers over to Holywell. Arriving at Histon, we are reminded that 2003 was the centenary of Unwins the seedsmen, whose business was started here in 1903. If the first half of our journey has been dominated by tourism, the second half is decidedly agricultural, with farming being the main rural occupation, and it is only as we arrive at Cambridge that we see signs of modern light industry.

HUNTINGDON
The Town Hall and Market Hill c1965 H136064

The Town Hall and magistrates' court still dominates Market Hill. It overlooks the recently refurbished Thinking Soldier war memorial, designed by Lady Kathleen Scott (widow of Captain Scott of the Antarctic) and erected in 1923. The new plinth includes an inscription commemorating those who fought in conflicts since 1945. The whole square was pedestrianised and paved in 2001, so parked cars are now a memory.

▲ HUNTINGDON
A Delivery Van c1955 H136019X

Boots and International Stores had both been long-term tenants of this corner, but in 1976 Boots moved away, and the Leeds Permanent Building Society, followed by the Halifax, moved in. Coleman's, the stationer's, took over in 2001. International Stores became a butcher's shop in the 1970s, and by 1983 the site was Savory & Moore, the chemists. It is now a Savers shop.

◄ HUNTINGDON
The High Street c1965 H136076

A careful look shows new tenants for many shops. On the right, the offices for the Jenkins & Jones Falcon Brewery have now been converted to flats, and the falcon statue has been restored. The range of shops beyond, including Osman's Ironmongery, are now estate agents, whilst on the other side of the street only the newsagents, now Jayes, keep the same trade.

HUNTINGDON
High Street c1955
H136002

The most striking change is the loss of Holy Trinity church with its tall spire, demolished in 1966. The site was sold to Tesco Ltd for £42,000 and Marks and Spencer refurbished the building in 2003. The Peterborough Co-operative drapery department (right) became the Gas Board, and is now a card shop.

▲ HUNTINGDON
The River c1960 H136036

This view facing the medieval bridge shows the boatyard in the foreground with the old stocking factory on the right and the bacon factory on the left. Although the bacon factory closed in the 1920s, the chimney remained until the 1970s when the new ring road was built. The factory on the right bank was turned into residential flats in the 1980s.

▶ GODMANCHESTER
Post Street c1955 G24023

This picture must have been taken from the middle of the main Huntingdon to Royston road at the junction with the road to the Offords. This view, towards Huntingdon, has changed little except that the garage has been replaced by a large car park with riverfront access.

GODMANCHESTER, *The Causeway c1955* G24016

On bright sunny days, this road becomes packed as people flock to enjoy a quiet stroll along the river. The Copper Kettle tearooms used to be near the Royal Oak (left), but it has now closed and two fast food shops have appeared. The Royal Oak is the sole surviving public house on the Causeway.

▶ **GODMANCHESTER**
The Causeway
c1955 G24041

This view of the old Causeway shows Cliffords the chemist's (extreme right) just before the shop closed. Part of this building now houses a fish and chip shop. In 1987 the local newspaper reported that the Causeway was reproduced in a model village outside Canberra in Australia!

◀ **GODMANCHESTER**
The Bridge c1955
G24007

The first Chinese Bridge on this site was built in 1827. Since then it has been replaced twice; the current wooden bridge dates from 1930, and was refurbished in 1979. Over the bridge is the Queen Elizabeth School dating from the 1500s and in use to 1947; it is now a public hall and meeting rooms.

▲ **GODMANCHESTER,** *The Causeway from the Park c1960* G24044

To reach the park we need to cross over the Chinese Bridge. The lake is actually the weir pool. This is a favourite venue for families, and with so many people using the park, bright red lifebelts are now placed along the water's edge.

HEMINGFORD GREY
Church Lane c1955
H408011

This view of River House (left), former home to local artist Dendy Sadler, has hardly changed - there is now a flagpole on the front and less greenery. To prevent accidents, a wall has been built along the riverbank and a small green provided as a turning point for vehicles.

HEMINGFORD GREY
High Street c1955 H408012

This view down the High Street towards St. Ives shows little change. The old post office (left) was turned into a bed & breakfast in the late 1960s, and the petrol pump disappeared about that time also. The new post office opened next door.

▲ **HEMINGFORD GREY**
The Village c1955 H408036

The Hemingford Laundry (left), which was taken over by the Huntingdon Model Laundry, closed in the late 1960s when Gordon Elphick opened a furniture shop on the premises. Further down on the left is the Society of the Resurrection's retreat, St Francis House.

◄ **HOUGHTON**
The Village c1960 H464006

This scene is timeless, except for the lack of traffic! This village is well known for its charming thatched cottages and historical connection to the Potto family, millers and nonconformists; a bronze memorial has been recently erected in the corner of the village square.

▶ **HOUGHTON**
*The Clock Tower
c1960* H464009

The clock tower, erected in 1902 in memory of George the son of Potto Brown, still provides shelter for visitors on their way to visit the famous mill or using the Ouse Valley Way. The water pump has been refurbished and joined by a telephone box, a cast iron sign and lamp posts.

◀**HOUGHTON**
The Mill c1960 H464005

This ancient mill was working up to the 1930s, when it was bought by the National Trust and run as a youth hostel. In 1980 renovation estimated at £11,000 was required, and it is now reinstated as a working mill. The caravan park beyond the millpond is still popular, with access to the Ouse Valley way via the white footbridge.

▲ **ST IVES,** *A Moped c1965* S23096X

Until the modern causeway was built in 1980, this medieval bridge provided the only crossing point over the River Ouse between Huntingdon and Earith. The chapel in the middle of the bridge, which was a pub in the 19th century and then a private house, is now open to visitors. It is strange how fashions come around again - the moped might well be seen today.

◄**ST IVES**
Bridge Street c1955 S23004

After a serious fire in 1975, the 18th-century building with the black cross facing us at the end of Bridge Street, formerly the Crown Inn, was demolished; this caused a major outcry. It was the last important old building to be removed in the town. Woolworth's now occupies the site, and has kept the cross on its facade.

ST IVES
Market Place c1955
S23030

Looking up the Market Place towards St Andrews Church in the distance, we see the statue of Oliver Cromwell, who farmed here briefly before the Civil War. Ramsey Abbey was granted an annual fair here in medieval times; the present day Monday Market is a reminder of those days.

ST IVES
Market Place c1955
S23008

Looking in the opposite direction to No S23030 (page 79), we can see on the right-hand site of the street two of the 48 public houses that could be found in the town in 1889. Both the Golden Lion and the Robin Hood are still trading, but the cycle shop (near right) has been replaced by a ladies' dress shop.

▶ **FENSTANTON**
*Chequer Street
c1955* F191003

We are looking away
from the High Street
down Chequer Street.
The post-enclosure
brick cottages on the
left have now been
replaced with modern
housing. In the
distance is the Manor
House, once home of
Lancelot 'Capability'
Brown, the famous
landscape gardener.

◀**FENSTANTON**
The Tudor Hotel c1965
F191013

This hotel became well
known in the 1970s when
it was associated with
Eric Morecambe (of
Morecambe and Wise
fame); more recently it
has become a Thai
restaurant, where I am
afraid you would need to
pay a little more for a
meal than the 8/6d
advertised in this
photograph!

▲ **HILTON,** *Potton Road c1955* H440010

This quiet village road is now a 'rat run' for motorists avoiding hold-ups on the A14. So frantic has the traffic become, that the second thatched cottage was hit by a lorry twice in one year, losing the corner wall and its thatch.

◀**HILTON**

The Village Hall c1955
H440023

After the village school closed in 1955, the building became the village hall. The famous turf maze, some 50 feet in diameter, is right beside the hall. The monument, topped by a finial (right), marks the centre, and records the death in 1729 of William Sparrow, the creator of the maze.

▼ **SWAVESEY,** *High Street c1965* S675011

Coming off the old A604, now the A14, the High Street meanders through Swavesey village for over a mile passing chapels, farm houses, cottages and 19th-century terraces - very little has changed here for generations.

▶ **SWAVESEY**

High Street c1965 S675019

The centre of the village is located around the White Horse public house (centre right). The baker's shop (extreme right) has gone, and is now called The Old Bakehouse, whilst the end portion has become a hairdresser's shop with windows inserted at ground and first floor level.

◄ **WILLINGHAM**
High Street c1955
W510023

The view down the High Street has changed very little, but the increased volume of traffic has brought traffic lights to the junction with the road to Over. A barber's shop has replaced the radio shop on the left, and the Willingham Auction Rooms now occupy the adjoining building.

► **WILLINGHAM**
The Black Bull c1955
W510009

This public house has changed very little - the white boarding is now black, and the poster for Greene King Harvest Brown Ale has gone. Patrons using the outside seating in what used to be the car park can now watch the traffic flow across this busy junction with the Over/Rampton road.

▲ **OVER,** *Fen Lane c1965* O114015

Fen Lane lives up to its name, with farm vehicles and horses being the main traffic. There has been some development here, with a new bungalow in the yard beside the Dutch-gabled Ivy House and a terrace of houses, dating from the 1970s, replacing the railings on the left.

► **OVER,** *The Mill c1965* O114011

This well-known landmark is the survivor of the two mills recorded in 1575. Originally a smock mill, and rebuilt as a tower mill, it fell into disrepair during the Second World War. It was then restored; by 1970, with just two sails, it was grinding organically grown wheat for a wholefood company.

▲ **HISTON,** *High Street c1965* H442004

Just past the Village Green, the Boot (left), one of the oldest pubs in the village, and the Barley Mow beyond, are both still trading, although the General Stores between them has been demolished to make a car park. This is one of the few villages where the post office (right) has survived intact.

CAMBRIDGE TOWN AND THE LOCAL AREA

Cambridge, probably best known for its university, is a pleasant town full of interesting corners and winding alleyways, all of which seem to end up at the river Cam. During term time the streets are filled with students on bicycles, most of whom have never heard of the highway code. Tourism is a major industry in Cambridge, with the usual rash of shops selling postcards, souvenirs and fast food, intermingled with academic bookshops, hotels and a large noisy market. The Strawberry Fayre each year, along with the Cambridge Folk Festival, attract a good following. The surrounding villages of Trumpington, Grantchester, Horningsea and Fulbourn all act as dormitories for Cambridge industry, centred on the new science parks on the outskirts of the town. The airport has also brought added employment to the area, which is one of the most prosperous in the eastern counties.

CAMBRIDGE
St John's College, the Tennis Courts c1955 C14016

A university tutor commented: 'No such serious games played here today! The tennis courts are elsewhere and the shorts are, probably, shorter, and there are girls!'

CAMBRIDGE
St John's College and Wren's Bridge c1955
C14021

Punting in a skirt- what fun! Wren's bridge, built by Robert Rumbold in 1709-12, has a balustraded parapet and heraldic beasts on display. It is also known as Kitchen Bridge; it seems that the master and fellows of St John's defied the architect and had it put at the end of the lane leading to the college kitchens.

▶ **CAMBRIDGE**
Kings College c1955
C14055

The magnificent view down the Parade has changed little over the years. Whilst the bicycles remain a common feature, cars have vanished with city centre pedestrianisation. The bollards of 2003 go up and down to control the traffic - the old ones disappeared years ago.

◀ **CAMBRIDGE**
Jesus College c1955
C14050

Since 1955 a new residential block has been built in the background of the picture, whilst a new library to the south of the chapel has appeared. Other new accommodation, to provide rooms on site for as many students as possible, has been added, although the Commons in the foreground and to the right are carefully preserved.

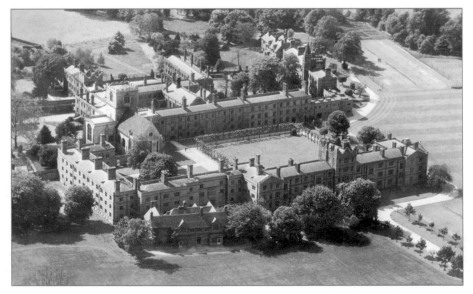

▲ **CAMBRIDGE,** *St John's College Chapel Tower c1955* C14015

The extension to Trinity College library is well hidden behind the willows, which also provide shade for the punters on this busy stretch of the river.

◄ **CAMBRIDGE**
The River Cam c1965
C14110

We are standing on Magdalene Bridge looking at the Cam. This is still one of the main punt hiring stations in Cambridge today, although the modern-day prices reflect the passage of time - at the time of this photograph, it cost 3s 6d to hire a punt and 3s a canoe. The quayside on the right was developed in 1985 for residential housing with shops and a wine bar.

CAMBRIDGE
*Trumpington Street
c1955* C14064

We have moved away from the river, and are looking down one of the main city streets; the scene nowadays has changed little. The traffic is now diverted down Silver Street (left), and the street lights have been replaced by the modern Richardson Candles.

▼ **HORNINGSEA,** *The Village c1955* H443007

The 16th century timber-framed Plough and Fleece public house on the left of the road was just one of the three pubs in the village. In the 19th century, it introduced limited opening hours when the coprolite diggers became rowdy. The opening of the Cambridge by-pass in 1978 unfortunately saw an increase in the traffic along this quiet road.

► **GRANTCHESTER**

The Rose and Crown c1965 G44018

The Rose and Crown, now the Rupert Brooke, has been extended at the front, losing the outside seating area. The change in name reflects the growing interest in Rupert Brooke, the First World War poet from this village. The nearby Grantchester Tea Rooms houses an excellent collection of photographs and exhibits about the poet and his contemporaries.

◄ GRANTCHESTER
High Street c1965
G44017

Other less literate residents of Grantchester are also remembered. Edward Wright, the village baker, gave his name to this row of cottages in the High Street. His house and the bakery, second from left, are thought to be more than 300 years old. The Cambridge Cottage Improvement Society bought them in 1938 for £150, and with a grant, Wrights Row was repaired and modernised. This scene has not changed at all in the past 45 years.

► GRANTCHESTER
The Red Lion c1965
G44022

Hidden away behind the Green Man Inn, the Red Lion is nowadays a popular, floodlit public house, painted a glowing orange but retaining the thatched roof. The delightful rampant lion sign (right) has now been replaced by a beer garden, and the enlarged car park is controlled by an automatic barrier.

▼ **GRANTCHESTER,** *Byron's Pool c1955* G44009

This haven of tranquillity lies just a quarter of a mile from the main road down a wooded path, but many people feel that it has been spoilt by concrete buttresses and notice boards. It is here that the poet Byron is said to have swum naked with a choirboy from Cambridge.

▶ **TRUMPINGTON**
Anstey Way c1960 T94024

At first glance, this row of modern shops, named after the local Anstey Hall, has not changed since 1960; but closer inspection reveals new tenants in the shops, larger trees and flower beds, and more people - the area is a popular haunt of the younger generation these days.

◄**TRUMPINGTON**
The War Memorial c1960 T94030

This magnificently carved war memorial stands at the junction of the Grantchester and Trumpington roads. The carvings on all four sides of the pillar were the work of Eric Gill. Alas, the public house opposite has long gone, to be replaced with a whole range of modern dwelling houses.

► **FULBOURN**
Cow Lane c1950
F104007

Cow Lane has changed in recent years, with infill building visible to the left of the house in the centre of this picture. The road has been repaved and kerbed with a pavement on each side - an indication of how busy this thoroughfare has become.

FULBOURN, *The Post Office c1950* F104013

The post office scene is virtually unchanged, except that the sun canopy has gone, and bicycle parking replaces the postbox under the cigarette advertisement, which has also vanished. One new addition to the modern scene is a parish council notice board between the gates and the shop front.

SOUTH AND EAST CAMBRIDGESHIRE

We start the final stage of our journey around Cambridgeshire just north of Cambridge off the A10 at Waterbeach, and then cut across the Adventurer's Fen, harking back to the 17th-century drainage works, through Wicken and on to Soham, and then turn south to Burwell. At Burwell we find the Devil's Dyke earthworks and a modern education centre where students of all ages gather. From Burwell we wander south to Swaffham Bulbeck, built on one of the lodes from the river Cam, and thence to Bottisham. Crossing the A14 we visit Great Shelford, Sawston and Stapleford, all providing dormitory accommodation for commuters working in both London and Cambridge. The countryside changes from open fenland with windswept vistas dotted with agricultural machinery to closed fields, hedges and picturesque thatched cottages. Heading south we come to Little Abingdon, home of one of the early land settlement schemes following the Depression years of the 1930s, and now with its own science park. We leave the county at Linton on the border with Essex.

WATERBEACH, *High Street c1955* W509011

In the 1960s two large housing estates were laid out on the east and west of the main street, and in 1972 a Village Society was formed to oppose the continued growth. The nearby airfield was used in World War II for bombers and then for training, with the 39 Regiment of Royal Engineers stationed here from 1966 onwards.

▶ **WATERBEACH**
Greenside c1960
W509035

The Green was the traditional site of the Feast, which featured a procession led by a brass band. This lapsed during the Second World War, and it was not until 1971 that a new headmaster revived the idea. The modern Feast is held in mid June, and from 1981 onwards has again featured local brass bands.

◀ **WATERBEACH**
The River Cam, Clayhithe c1955
W509003

The Clayhithe ferry ceased operating in 1875 when a company was formed to replace it with an iron bridge to be maintained by tolls. The Cam Sailing Boat and Motor Boat clubs now use the old moorings.

▲ **WATERBEACH,** *The Bridge Hotel, Clayhithe c1960* W509019

Originally called the House of Lords, this public house was enlarged by the Bridge Company when the ferry closed. It was renamed the Clayhithe Ferry in the 1880s, and by 1916 had become a hotel. Steamboats bringing visitors to the Feast stopped here in the 1890s.

◄ **WICKEN**
North Street c1955
W493024

The sign on the left is a sad reminder of the old village school. Although enlarged in 1974, it was threatened with closure in 1978, and after loosing eight teachers in sixteen years, finally closed in 1992 when there were only 35 pupils on the register. The school was sold for conversion to a private dwelling.

WICKEN, *The Pond c1955* W493007

We continue on to the village pond, which now has a fringe of
sedge and reeds and is home to many coot, duck and moorhen. The
old thatched house on the left was replaced in 1959 by a modern
house. Nearby is Wicken Fen, a major wetland conservation area
covering 330 acres owned by the National Trust.

SOHAM, *Churchgate Street c1955* S597005

Of the two public houses shown here on the wide main street leading up to St Andrew's church, only the Fountain (centre right), originally known as the Crown and rebuilt after a fire in 1900, is still trading. The Crown Hotel (left) became a private dwelling house when the licensees Mr and Mrs Charles Bullen retired in the late 1960s.

▶ **SOHAM**
Stillyards c1955
S597016

In the foreground is the hoist for the still yard or steelyard - a device for weighing wagons - dating from the 18th century and now a listed building. It stands in Fountain Lane, behind the Fountain Inn.

◀ **SOHAM**
Brook Dam c1955
S597023

Soham is the largest parish outside the Isle of Ely, and is surrounded by fenland. The Brook Dam was probably so named in the 17th century when the lower portion of the Snail River was diverted by a dam as part of the major drainage works.

▲ **BURWELL,** *High Street c1955* B728025

Fortunately the past 45 years have not changed this scene. The David Smith factory (corrugated packaging) in the distance has now moved to Newmarket, and the old malthouse with the rounded roof (centre) is now an office building with a car park alongside. Behind the trees is the sports field.

◄ **BURWELL**
The Sports Club c1955
B728038

This pavilion was built by the David Smith factory alongside the cricket pitch. When the factory moved to Newmarket, there was some debate about the future of the sports field; whilst the debate was successfully resolved, the pavilion declined, and is now derelict. A modern sports club has been built overlooking the cricket field.

▶ BURWELL
The Mill c1955 B728009K

The old mill is now a landmark for the Museum of Fenland Life, which is situated in the old barns alongside. The vegetable plots shown beside the track have been built over with houses, giving the appearance of a cul-de-sac, and the visitor is pleasantly surprised to find the museum right under the mill.

▼ SWAFFHAM BULBECK
The Mill c1955 S678013

This mill at Commercial End with its attached buildings started to decay in the 1930s, and by 1955 the last barge was sunk in the old fishpond. The water channels were filled in by the 1970s. One granary was converted to offices in the 1980s, and the remainder is being used as a pottery.

▶ SWAFFHAM BULBECK
Lordship Farm c1955
S678015

This imposing late 18th-century farmhouse, incorporating some earlier building, was listed Grade II in December 1951. This picture shows the replacement 20th-century windows, which nowadays would not be permitted in such a delightful period building.

◄ **BOTTISHAM**
High Street c1955
B727005

This view shows the High Street just before the development of the 1960s, when about 200 new houses were built off the High Street behind the trees. The sewage works, which had begun in the 1950s, were finally completed by 1964, opening the way for further expansion.

▼ **GREAT SHELFORD,** *High Street c1955* G278009

In the late 1980s the Black Swan public house (left) was demolished; the land became a used car lot, attached to a garage (just out of the picture on the left). At about the same time the Peacock Inn beyond became a private house, and the telephone box (left) was moved across the street.

▶ **SAWSTON**

The Village c1965 S671017

The Greyhound public house is one of the few buildings on this side of the street to have remained unchanged. The garage (left) beyond Queens Road, now owned by Vindis, has expanded, and traffic calming measures have attempted to slow down the local traffic.

◄ **SAWSTON**
High Street c1965
S671003

This view looking back towards the Greyhound shows the High Street before the major developments of the 1980s and 1990s. The Co-op (left) now houses a fish and chip shop, and the small garage (right) just down from the Fox pub has gone, to be replaced by modern shops.

▶ **STAPLEFORD**
The Parish Church c1960 S751001

Over the past forty years there have been some dramatic internal changes to St Andrew's Church. A new east window by Christopher Webb and a statue of St Andrew by John Skelton appeared in the1960s. In 1988 a tile maze was created from the centre of the west wall to the font, and a new organ was dedicated.

▶ **STAPLEFORD**
The County Primary School c1965
S751009

Now the Stapleford Community School, the original red brick school was opened in 1878, and the building has been extended several times since. The original schoolhouse was converted to a hostel for pupils of the adjacent Green Hedges School for handicapped children.

◀**LITTLE ABINGTON**
Jeremiah's Tea House c1965 L527008a

A favourite place to visit from Cambridge in the early 20th century, this well known teahouse disappeared in the 1970s, along with the two village pubs, the Prince of Wales (adjoining the teahouse) and the Crown. The village now boasts a general store, a pottery with coffee shop and two garages with a cafe.

▲ **LITTLE ABINGTON,** *The Church c1965* L527009

St Mary's Church, built of field stones and dressed with ashlar, was thoroughly restored in 1885. According to a survey of 1973, the church owned a paten dating from 1728 and a paten and cup from 1828. Of the three bells in 1552, only one survives today.

◀ **LINTON,** *High Street c1955* L459049

The High Street today looks much the same as it did in the 1950s - except that like so many small towns, the shops have gone. Barclays Bank (left) closed in 1998, and the grocer's shop, then International Stores and finally Gateway, closed in 1983 and is now private housing.

▲ **LINTON**
The Church c1955 L459022

In 1897 the vicar employed district visitors to serve the growing congregation, estimated at 1,200 people with 240 regular communicants. In 1959 the congregation had shrunk to around 11. Since this picture was taken the trees around the church have grown, and it cannot be seen from this tree by the brook.

► **LINTON**
A Clappers Stile c1955 L459013

A possible relict from the 19th century enclosure, this stile was rebuilt in 1998, but the gate has now gone. When this picture was taken in the 1950s, the Linton estate farms were mainly arable, with only 200 acres recorded as grassland.

INDEX

Frith Book Co Titles

www.francisfrith.co.uk

The Frith Book Company publishes over 100 new titles each year. A selection of those currently available is listed below. For latest catalogue please contact Frith Book Co.
Town Books 96 pages, approximately 100 photos. **County and Themed Books** 128 pages, approximately 150 photos (unless specified). All titles hardback with laminated case and jacket, except those indicated pb (paperback)

Amersham, Chesham & Rickmansworth (pb)	1-85937-340-2	£9.99	Devon (pb)	1-85937-297-x	£9.99
Andover (pb)	1-85937-292-9	£9.99	Devon Churches (pb)	1-85937-250-3	£9.99
Aylesbury (pb)	1-85937-227-9	£9.99	Dorchester (pb)	1-85937-307-0	£9.99
Barnstaple (pb)	1-85937-300-3	£9.99	Dorset (pb)	1-85937-269-4	£9.99
Basildon Living Memories (pb)	1-85937-515-4	£9.99	Dorset Coast (pb)	1-85937-299-6	£9.99
Bath (pb)	1-85937-419-0	£9.99	Dorset Living Memories (pb)	1-85937-584-7	£9.99
Bedford (pb)	1-85937-205-8	£9.99	Down the Severn (pb)	1-85937-560-x	£9.99
Bedfordshire Living Memories	1-85937-513-8	£14.99	Down The Thames (pb)	1-85937-278-3	£9.99
Belfast (pb)	1-85937-303-8	£9.99	Down the Trent	1-85937-311-9	£14.99
Berkshire (pb)	1-85937-191-4	£9.99	East Anglia (pb)	1-85937-265-1	£9.99
Berkshire Churches	1-85937-170-1	£17.99	East Grinstead (pb)	1-85937-138-8	£9.99
Berkshire Living Memories	1-85937-332-1	£14.99	East London	1-85937-080-2	£14.99
Black Country	1-85937-497-2	£12.99	East Sussex (pb)	1-85937-606-1	£9.99
Blackpool (pb)	1-85937-393-3	£9.99	Eastbourne (pb)	1-85937-399-2	£9.99
Bognor Regis (pb)	1-85937-431-x	£9.99	Edinburgh (pb)	1-85937-193-0	£8.99
Bournemouth (pb)	1-85937-545-6	£9.99	England In The 1880s	1-85937-331-3	£17.99
Bradford (pb)	1-85937-204-x	£9.99	Essex - Second Selection	1-85937-456-5	£14.99
Bridgend (pb)	1-85937-386-0	£7.99	Essex (pb)	1-85937-270-8	£9.99
Bridgwater (pb)	1-85937-305-4	£9.99	Essex Coast	1-85937-342-9	£14.99
Bridport (pb)	1-85937-327-5	£9.99	Essex Living Memories	1-85937-490-5	£14.99
Brighton (pb)	1-85937-192-2	£8.99	Exeter	1-85937-539-1	£9.99
Bristol (pb)	1-85937-264-3	£9.99	Exmoor (pb)	1-85937-608-8	£9.99
British Life A Century Ago (pb)	1-85937-213-9	£9.99	Falmouth (pb)	1-85937-594-4	£9.99
Buckinghamshire (pb)	1-85937-200-7	£9.99	Folkestone (pb)	1-85937-124-8	£9.99
Camberley (pb)	1-85937-222-8	£9.99	Frome (pb)	1-85937-317-8	£9.99
Cambridge (pb)	1-85937-422-0	£9.99	Glamorgan	1-85937-488-3	£14.99
Cambridgeshire (pb)	1-85937-420-4	£9.99	Glasgow (pb)	1-85937-190-6	£9.99
Cambridgeshire Villages	1-85937-523-5	£14.99	Glastonbury (pb)	1-85937-338-0	£7.99
Canals And Waterways (pb)	1-85937-291-0	£9.99	Gloucester (pb)	1-85937-232-5	£9.99
Canterbury Cathedral (pb)	1-85937-179-5	£9.99	Gloucestershire (pb)	1-85937-561-8	£9.99
Cardiff (pb)	1-85937-093-4	£9.99	Great Yarmouth (pb)	1-85937-426-3	£9.99
Carmarthenshire (pb)	1-85937-604-5	£9.99	Greater Manchester (pb)	1-85937-266-x	£9.99
Chelmsford (pb)	1-85937-310-0	£9.99	Guildford (pb)	1-85937-410-7	£9.99
Cheltenham (pb)	1-85937-095-0	£9.99	Hampshire (pb)	1-85937-279-1	£9.99
Cheshire (pb)	1-85937-271-6	£9.99	Harrogate (pb)	1-85937-423-9	£9.99
Chester (pb)	1-85937-382 8	£9.99	Hastings and Bexhill (pb)	1-85937-131-0	£9.99
Chesterfield (pb)	1-85937-378-x	£9.99	Heart of Lancashire (pb)	1-85937-197-3	£9.99
Chichester (pb)	1-85937-228-7	£9.99	Helston (pb)	1-85937-214-7	£9.99
Churches of East Cornwall (pb)	1-85937-249-x	£9.99	Hereford (pb)	1-85937-175-2	£9.99
Churches of Hampshire (pb)	1-85937-207-4	£9.99	Herefordshire (pb)	1-85937-567-7	£9.99
Cinque Ports & Two Ancient Towns	1-85937-492-1	£14.99	Herefordshire Living Memories	1-85937-514-6	£14.99
Colchester (pb)	1-85937-188-4	£8.99	Hertfordshire (pb)	1-85937-247-3	£9.99
Cornwall (pb)	1-85937-229-5	£9.99	Horsham (pb)	1-85937-432-8	£9.99
Cornwall Living Memories	1-85937-248-1	£14.99	Humberside (pb)	1-85937-605-3	£9.99
Cotswolds (pb)	1-85937-230-9	£9.99	Hythe, Romney Marsh, Ashford (pb)	1-85937-256-2	£9.99
Cotswolds Living Memories	1-85937-255-4	£14.99	Ipswich (pb)	1-85937-424-7	£9.99
County Durham (pb)	1-85937-398-4	£9.99	Isle of Man (pb)	1-85937-268-6	£9.99
Croydon Living Memories (pb)	1-85937-162-0	£9.99	Isle of Wight (pb)	1-85937-429-8	£9.99
Cumbria (pb)	1-85937-621-5	£9.99	Isle of Wight Living Memories	1-85937-304-6	£14.99
Derby (pb)	1-85937-367-4	£9.99	Kent (pb)	1-85937-189-2	£9.99
Derbyshire (pb)	1-85937-196-5	£9.99	Kent Living Memories(pb)	1-85937-401-8	£9.99
Derbyshire Living Memories	1-85937-330-5	£14.99	Kings Lynn (pb)	1-85937-334-8	£9.99

Available from your local bookshop or from the publisher

Frith Book Co Titles (continued)

Title	ISBN	Price	Title	ISBN	Price
Lake District (pb)	1-85937-275-9	£9.99	Sherborne (pb)	1-85937-301-1	£9.99
Lancashire Living Memories	1-85937-335-6	£14.99	Shrewsbury (pb)	1-85937-325-9	£9.99
Lancaster, Morecambe, Heysham (pb)	1-85937-233-3	£9.99	Shropshire (pb)	1-85937-326-7	£9.99
Leeds (pb)	1-85937-202-3	£9.99	Shropshire Living Memories	1-85937-643-6	£14.99
Leicester (pb)	1-85937-381-x	£9.99	Somerset	1-85937-153-1	£14.99
Leicestershire & Rutland Living Memories	1-85937-500-6	£12.99	South Devon Coast	1-85937-107-8	£14.99
Leicestershire (pb)	1-85937-185-x	£9.99	South Devon Living Memories (pb)	1-85937-609-6	£9.99
Lighthouses	1-85937-257-0	£9.99	South East London (pb)	1-85937-263-5	£9.99
Lincoln (pb)	1-85937-380-1	£9.99	South Somerset	1-85937-318-6	£14.99
Lincolnshire (pb)	1-85937-433-6	£9.99	South Wales	1-85937-519-7	£14.99
Liverpool and Merseyside (pb)	1-85937-234-1	£9.99	Southampton (pb)	1-85937-427-1	£9.99
London (pb)	1-85937-183-3	£9.99	Southend (pb)	1-85937-313-5	£9.99
London Living Memories	1-85937-454-9	£14.99	Southport (pb)	1-85937-425-5	£9.99
Ludlow (pb)	1-85937-176-0	£9.99	St Albans (pb)	1-85937-341-0	£9.99
Luton (pb)	1-85937-235-x	£9.99	St Ives (pb)	1-85937-415-8	£9.99
Maidenhead (pb)	1-85937-339-9	£9.99	Stafford Living Memories (pb)	1-85937-503-0	£9.99
Maidstone (pb)	1-85937-391-7	£9.99	Staffordshire (pb)	1-85937-308-9	£9.99
Manchester (pb)	1-85937-198-1	£9.99	Stourbridge (pb)	1-85937-530-8	£9.99
Marlborough (pb)	1-85937-336-4	£9.99	Stratford upon Avon (pb)	1-85937-388-7	£9.99
Middlesex	1-85937-158-2	£14.99	Suffolk	1-85937-221-x	£9.99
Monmouthshire	1-85937-532-4	£14.99	Suffolk Coast (pb)	1-85937-610-x	£9.99
New Forest (pb)	1-85937-390-9	£9.99	Surrey (pb)	1-85937-240-6	£9.99
Newark (pb)	1-85937-366-6	£9.99	Surrey Living Memories	1-85937-328-3	£14.99
Newport, Wales (pb)	1-85937-258-9	£9.99	Sussex (pb)	1-85937-184-1	£9.99
Newquay (pb)	1-85937-421-2	£9.99	Sutton (pb)	1-85937-337-2	£9.99
Norfolk (pb)	1-85937-195-7	£9.99	Swansea (pb)	1-85937-167-1	£9.99
Norfolk Broads	1-85937-486-7	£14.99	Taunton (pb)	1-85937-314-3	£9.99
Norfolk Living Memories (pb)	1-85937-402-6	£9.99	Tees Valley & Cleveland (pb)	1-85937-623-1	£9.99
North Buckinghamshire	1-85937-626-6	£14.99	Teignmouth (pb)	1-85937-370-4	£7.99
North Devon Living Memories	1-85937-261-9	£14.99	Thanet (pb)	1-85937-116-7	£9.99
North Hertfordshire	1-85937-547-2	£14.99	Tiverton (pb)	1-85937-178-7	£9.99
North London (pb)	1-85937-403-4	£9.99	Torbay (pb)	1-85937-597-9	£9.99
North Somerset	1-85937-302-x	£14.99	Truro (pb)	1-85937-598-7	£9.99
North Wales (pb)	1-85937-298-8	£9.99	Victorian & Edwardian Dorset	1-85937-254-6	£14.99
North Yorkshire (pb)	1-85937-236-8	£9.99	Victorian & Edwardian Kent (pb)	1-85937-624-X	£9.99
Northamptonshire Living Memories	1-85937-529-4	£14.99	Victorian & Edwardian Maritime Album (pb)	1-85937-622-3	£9.99
Northamptonshire	1-85937-150-7	£14.99	Victorian and Edwardian Sussex (pb)	1-85937-625-8	£9.99
Northumberland Tyne & Wear (pb)	1-85937-281-3	£9.99	Villages of Devon (pb)	1-85937-293-7	£9.99
Northumberland	1-85937-522-7	£14.99	Villages of Kent (pb)	1-85937-294-5	£9.99
Norwich (pb)	1-85937-194-9	£8.99	Villages of Sussex (pb)	1-85937-295-3	£9.99
Nottingham (pb)	1-85937-324-0	£9.99	Warrington (pb)	1-85937-507-3	£9.99
Nottinghamshire (pb)	1-85937-187-6	£9.99	Warwick (pb)	1-85937-518-9	£9.99
Oxford (pb)	1-85937-411-5	£9.99	Warwickshire (pb)	1-85937-203-1	£9.99
Oxfordshire (pb)	1-85937-430-1	£9.99	Welsh Castles (pb)	1-85937-322-4	£9.99
Oxfordshire Living Memories	1-85937-525-1	£14.99	West Midlands (pb)	1-85937-289-9	£9.99
Paignton (pb)	1-85937-374-7	£7.99	West Sussex (pb)	1-85937-607-x	£9.99
Peak District (pb)	1-85937-280-5	£9.99	West Yorkshire (pb)	1-85937-201-5	£9.99
Pembrokeshire	1-85937-262-7	£14.99	Weston Super Mare (pb)	1-85937-306-2	£9.99
Penzance (pb)	1-85937-595-2	£9.99	Weymouth (pb)	1-85937-209-0	£9.99
Peterborough (pb)	1-85937-219-8	£9.99	Wiltshire (pb)	1-85937-277-5	£9.99
Picturesque Harbours	1-85937-208-2	£14.99	Wiltshire Churches (pb)	1-85937-171-x	£9.99
Piers	1-85937-237-6	£17.99	Wiltshire Living Memories (pb)	1-85937-396-8	£9.99
Plymouth (pb)	1-85937-389-5	£9.99	Winchester (pb)	1-85937-428-x	£9.99
Poole & Sandbanks (pb)	1-85937-251-1	£9.99	Windsor (pb)	1-85937-333-x	£9.99
Preston (pb)	1-85937-212-0	£9.99	Wokingham & Bracknell (pb)	1-85937-329-1	£9.99
Reading (pb)	1-85937-238-4	£9.99	Woodbridge (pb)	1-85937-498-0	£9.99
Redhill to Reigate (pb)	1-85937-596-0	£9.99	Worcester (pb)	1-85937-165-5	£9.99
Ringwood (pb)	1-85937-384-4	£7.99	Worcestershire Living Memories	1-85937-489-1	£14.99
Romford (pb)	1-85937-319-4	£9.99	Worcestershire	1-85937-152-3	£14.99
Royal Tunbridge Wells (pb)	1-85937-504-9	£9.99	York (pb)	1-85937-199-x	£9.99
Salisbury (pb)	1-85937-239-2	£9.99	Yorkshire (pb)	1-85937-186-8	£9.99
Scarborough (pb)	1-85937-379-8	£9.99	Yorkshire Coastal Memories	1-85937-506-5	£14.99
Sevenoaks and Tonbridge (pb)	1-85937-392-5	£9.99	Yorkshire Dales	1-85937-502-2	£14.99
Sheffield & South Yorks (pb)	1-85937-267-8	£9.99	Yorkshire Living Memories (pb)	1-85937-397-6	£9.99

See Frith books on the internet at www.francisfrith.co.uk

FRITH PRODUCTS & SERVICES

Francis Frith would doubtless be pleased to know that the pioneering publishing venture he started in 1860 still continues today. Over a hundred and forty years later, The Francis Frith Collection continues in the same innovative tradition and is now one of the foremost publishers of vintage photographs in the world. Some of the current activities include:

Interior Decoration

Today Frith's photographs can be seen framed and as giant wall murals in thousands of pubs, restaurants, hotels, banks, retail stores and other public buildings throughout the country. In every case they enhance the unique local atmosphere of the places they depict and provide reminders of gentler days in an increasingly busy and frenetic world.

Product Promotions

Frith products are used by many major companies to promote the sales of their own products or to reinforce their own history and heritage. Frith promotions have been used by Hovis bread, Courage beers, Scots Porage Oats, Colman's mustard, Cadbury's foods, Mellow Birds coffee, Dunhill pipe tobacco, Guinness, and Bulmer's Cider.

Genealogy and Family History

As the interest in family history and roots grows world-wide, more and more people are turning to Frith's photographs of Great Britain for images of the towns, villages and streets where their ancestors lived; and, of course, photographs of the churches and chapels where their ancestors were christened, married and buried are an essential part of every genealogy tree and family album.

Frith Products

All Frith photographs are available Framed or just as Mounted Prints and Posters (size 23 x 16 inches). These may be ordered from the address below. From time to time other products - Address Books, Calendars, Table Mats, etc - are available.

The Internet

Already fifty thousand Frith photographs can be viewed and purchased on the internet through the Frith websites and a myriad of partner sites.

For more detailed information on Frith companies and products, look at these sites:

www.francisfrith.co.uk
www.francisfrith.com
(for North American visitors)

See the complete list of Frith Books at:

www.francisfrith.co.uk

This web site is regularly updated with the latest list of publications from the Frith Book Company. If you wish to buy books relating to another part of the country that your local bookshop does not stock, you may purchase on-line.

For further information, trade, or author enquiries please contact us at the address below:
The Francis Frith Collection, Frith's Barn, Teffont, Salisbury, Wiltshire, England SP3 5QP.
Tel: +44 (0)1722 716 376 Fax: +44 (0)1722 716 881 Email: sales@francisfrith.co.uk

---

See Frith books on the internet at www.francisfrith.co.uk

FREE MOUNTED PRINT

Mounted Print
Overall size 14 x 11 inches

Fill in and cut out this voucher and return
it with your remittance for £2.25 (to cover postage and handling). Offer valid for delivery to UK addresses only.

Choose any photograph included in this book.
Your SEPIA print will be A4 in size. It will be mounted in a cream mount with a burgundy rule line (overall size 14 x 11 inches).

**Order additional Mounted Prints
at HALF PRICE (only £7.49 each*)**
If you would like to order more Frith prints from this book, possibly as gifts for friends and family, you can buy them at half price (with no additional postage and handling costs).

Have your Mounted Prints framed
For an extra £14.95 per print* you can have your mounted print(s) framed in an elegant polished wood and gilt moulding, overall size 16 x 13 inches (no additional postage and handling required).

---

* IMPORTANT!

These special prices are only available if you order at the same time as you order your free mounted print. You must use the ORIGINAL VOUCHER on this page (no copies permitted). We can only despatch to one address.

Send completed Voucher form to:
The Francis Frith Collection, Frith's Barn, Teffont, Salisbury, Wiltshire SP3 5QP

Please do not photocopy this voucher. Only the original is valid, so please fill it in, cut it out and return it to us with your order.

Picture ref no	Page no	Qty	Mounted @ £7.49	Framed + £14.95	Total Cost
		1	Free of charge*	£	£
			£7.49	£	£
			£7.49	£	£
			£7.49	£	£
			£7.49	£	£
			£7.49	£	£

Please allow 28 days for delivery

* Post & handling (UK)	£2.25
Total Order Cost	£

Title of this book . . . .

I enclose a cheque/postal order for £ . . . .
made payable to 'The Francis Frith Collection'

OR please debit my Mastercard / Visa / Switch / Amex card
(credit cards please on all overseas orders), details below

Card Number

Issue No (Switch only)   Valid from (Amex/Switch)

Expires   Signature

Name Mr/Mrs/Ms ....

Address ....

....

....

.... Postcode ....

Daytime Tel No ....

Email ....

Valid to 31/12/05

Would you like to find out more about Francis Frith?

We have recently recruited some entertaining speakers who are happy to visit local groups, clubs and societies to give an illustrated talk documenting Frith's travels and photographs. If you are a member of such a group and are interested in hosting a presentation, we would love to hear from you.

Our speakers bring with them a small selection of our local town and county books, together with sample prints. They are happy to take orders. A small proportion of the order value is donated to the group who have hosted the presentation. The talks are therefore an excellent way of fundraising for small groups and societies.

Can you help us with information about any of the Frith photographs in this book?

We are gradually compiling an historical record for each of the photographs in the Frith archive. It is always fascinating to find out the names of the people shown in the pictures, as well as insights into the shops, buildings and other features depicted.

If you recognize anyone in the photographs in this book, or if you have information not already included in the author's caption, do let us know. We would love to hear from you, and will try to publish it in future books or articles.

Our production team

Frith books are produced by a small dedicated team at offices in the converted Grade II listed 18th-century barn at Teffont near Salisbury, illustrated above. Most have worked with the Frith Collection for many years. All have in common one quality: they have a passion for the Frith Collection. The team is constantly expanding, but currently includes:

Jason Buck, John Buck, Ruth Butler, Heather Crisp, David Davies, Isobel Hall, Julian Hight, Peter Horne, James Kinnear, Karen Kinnear, Tina Leary, Stuart Login, Amanda Lowe, David Marsh, Sue Molloy, Kate Rotondetto, Dean Scource, Eliza Sackett, Terence Sackett, Sandra Sampson, Adrian Sanders, Sandra Sanger, Julia Skinner, Claire Tarrier, Lewis Taylor, Shelley Tolcher and Lorraine Tuck.